The Raving Fortune

Noelle Kocot

Four Way Books
New York City

Distributed by
University Press
of New England
Hanover and
London

Please direct all inquiries to:

Editorial Office
Four Way Books
POB 535, Village Station
New York, NY 10014
www.fourwaybooks.com

Library of Congress Catalogue Card Number: 2002116857

ISBN: 1-884800-55-6

Cover art: Jennifer Kaufman

This book is manufactured in the United States of America and printed on acid-free paper.

Four Way Books is a division of Friends of Writers, Inc., a Vermont-based not-for-profit organization. We are grateful for the assistance we receive from individual donors and private foundations.

Distributed by University Press of New England
One Court Street, Lebanon, NH 03766

The Raving Fortune

Previously published:

4

Acknowledgments

Grateful acknowledgment is made to the following publications:

6500: "*Furor Poeticus,*" "The Map"
Anodyne: "Clothing"
Another Chicago Magazine: "There is a Tiara Dripping from the Skylights," "Consolations Before an Affair, Upper West Side," "A Lived Experience"
Barrow Street: "Over, Under, Through, With," "Poem Written in 17 Minutes," "Two Poems for Franz Wright"
Boog City: "Evening with the Financial Report"
The Brooklyn Rail: "Blankness, Much"
The Brooklyn Review: "I Don't Think I'll Ever Write This Poem"
Cello Entry: "*Sprich Auch Du,*" "The Planning of a Park," "From Bellevue Aquarium"
Conduit: "The Newlyweds and the Funny Papers," "The Whole Arcana from the Fool to the World"
East Village Online: "Love, Alters, Everything"
Fence: "The Raving Fortune," "Rushing Through the House I Behold the Numinous Dark of Forks, The Light-Bearing Phenomenology of Sunrise"
Fort Necessity: "Passing Over Water," "A Sure Sign That I've Been Here," "Try Anyway," "Civilization Day"
Lit: "Horse Sense and the Evolving Breeze," "I'm the Church You Should Go To More Often But Don't"
LUNGFULL!: "Beginner's Mind and Purple Plants," "The Face I Had Before I Was Born" "Ground Zero, Union Street Subway Station, August 1997"
New American Writing: "To the Place in My Head Where Ideas Come From:," "The Maddest Kind of Love," "Rondeau," "I Refuse to Wear Life Like a Loose Garment"

The poem "Consolations Before An Affair, Upper West Side" was reprinted in *Best American Poetry 2001.*

The poem, "To the Place In My Head Where Ideas Come From:," was made into a short film by filmmaker Joshua Mosely.

Special thanks is given to the National Endowment for the Arts and The Fund for Poetry for grants received, which made it possible for me to more peacefully do my work.

Much gratitude is given to the following individuals who supported me artistically, emotionally and spiritually while I wrote the poems included in this collection: Brenda Hillman, Chris Stroffolino, Curtis McCartney, Damon Tomblin, David Shapiro, Denise Duhamel, Franz Wright, Joanna Fuhrman, Joe Juracek, John Schertzer, Joshua Beckman, Joshua Clover, Martha Rhodes, Matt Rohrer, Lizzette Potthoff, Lou Asekoff, Patrick Donnelly, Rebecca Reilly, Rick Snyder, Soraya Shalforoosh, Steve Berg and Zach Saunders.

This collection is dedicated to Damon Tomblin.

Contents

III

The prayer of a couple whose hearts are united has the same value as the prayer of a great gathering of believers.

– Bahram Elahi

But all this flesh is only beginnings, and absences, absences, absences...

– Antonin Artaud

I

To the Place in My Head Where Ideas Come From:

While the soul traverses endless bouts of space,
The nihilist commits suicide over and over.
Ah to be young and vicious!
Ah to be old and viscous!
A giant living room stands between us
Lyric, Lyric
Somewhere a tree falls upon my life
(I.e., the time-abandoned balloon of sense,
The soft facts of my debasement),
And the sky, like a giant rubber glove, overarching it all,
Points to the dreary auscultations that die in sleep.

The beauty of it?
What on earth is the beauty of it?

It's the funeral inside the pretzel,
The cozy metamusic in which I, refulgent, say:
How the hell are you anyway?

A violin swings in the rain.
—Hey that's cheap.
—No *you* are, chasing the party that will never happen,
A shiny ball stapled onto infinity
As if you want to leave no part of the multiverse untouched.

But energy erases itself, see,
It's us against tomorrow, see,
Prodding our palms for some inheritance.
And the bereft assurances know nothing of the age,
Or if I can speak you into existence in some familiar way.

For now, all is as it should be:
The sky swells with xylophonic adornment,
The bow floats on the violin like a bee,

The escape hatch is filled to bursting with raw meat.

Anyway, how the *hell* are you?
Let me know, all right?

Yours Idiomatically,

The Sunnyside

Passing Over Water

The sunset is blinding today.
The bridge seems to have shed its cables,
And everything tapers to a methodical hissing, a calm.
I cannot hear above the wheels that softly sing

What seems a lullaby to soothe all of creation,
Meant to reach even into the rich marrow of stars.
I dreamed this once,
The bridge, the sea, the song of the train,

And in the dream there were fluorescent trees,
Fuchsia, bright yellow, electric teal,
Brushing against the sky in the breeze like fiber-optic lamps.
In the dream there was a feeling of utter silence,

Palpable as sketches for buildings,
And I wondered when it would leave, if it would leave at all,
Or if it would exist only in the prism of that instant
Where earlier I'd heard a voice urging me

Through an anguished mesh of faces and rain:
Forget everything you know, it is of no use to anyone,
And your ominous conjectures will shrivel away
In the salt of your own affliction.

I remember I sat in my seat just as I am now sitting,
Whispering over and over *dark is right, dark is right,*
And when I turned my face to the clear, dark window
I saw lions struggling to climb out of the sea.

I Am the Supernova of Your Psalmistry

The riding airiness of a shoelace speaks volumes
And peters out into an old chaos of the sun
In which we live. Joanna, I mean it
When I tell you that the interstices of protoplasm
Reek of nothing, oh nothing. I fall into romantic
Despoir so easily about art, and you dear
Child of the wild synapses and phonemes
Gone awry, child of narcissistic desire out of which
Things Get Made, you "apply lipstick to a Burmese cat"
While others look on smiling as they would
At a 5th grader applying a bandage to an unbruised knee,
Perfectly. I, too, hate it when things aren't finished.
I don't like poetry, poems, or poets lately,
Yet I get excited so easily when lines come to me:
I am the supernova of your psalmistry.
I want to scream with aggravated pleasure
Like the woman with the pierced clit in the porno flick.
The images stand at attention at my fingertips,
But I want none of it, I want to say I am 17
And have quit writing poetry to go to business school,
That there is nothing, oh nothing to imagine anymore,
Everything has been said and done a googol of times,
Yet I write this still with far flung steps
And yes, I crumpled miles of streets beneath
Our snowy feet as, together, we slid across the threshold
Of an age to smash the old Rosetta Stone.

Blankness, Much

Hot air blows on the 48th parallel of my ________.
Saltatory/no saltatory
Blankness, much.
And green is the way of my favorite oxen
Stored by the still
Still by the store
And green is the way.
Theoretically I rise up from the greenness of the world.
I catch birds falling out of trees.
In rage I crack broomsticks
On the lightning bolts of the Creator
Who breathes into me the slow strangulation
Of what was as hot air blows.
And the shards of music I strain to hear
Are bandaged now in a tidy heap,
Yet I rise up to catch them in embarrassing greenness
I rise up to catch them in embarrassing greenness
And commit them Lord, blankly, into your tattered green hands.

There is a Tiara Dripping from the Skylights

There is a tiara dripping from the skylights.
There is a saint who loves someone dead beneath my feet.
There is the X*O*X*O of my conscious breath,
And we are on the same page, the fine nature of it.

Somewhere an acoustic glacier silts across the grimace of a hearth.
There is gingham. Daguerreotypes. There is courtesy.
Laboratories pace away
In an obscure odyssey of preserved moccasins.

They seem to have misplaced their stilts.
And it's all so la-di-da, the aureate bootleg,
The helium brocade of a larger, stinging scent.
Over there are a lot of imperfect people

Loaded up with seashells, whistling from piazzas.
If they flay me, I will become a doe dipping my nose in beachy wine.
Can't you see how hard I'm trying?
But it's this tiara, this damned tiara,

The saint, the pages…
In theory, it is also the tobacco skylights,
The wizened xylophone cracked across the firmament
That tinks out and out, *it's no good to spend so much time alone.*

Walking in the Light

for Martha

The great sea in me is the same
As the sea's great weight
Around my neck.

Grant me rough edges.

Grant me the ghosts of merciful women
Until I realize what is lost is actually lost forever.

A fire is beginning to grow and sing
Its dark art,
Whispering curses, weaving spells,

And rising,

Rising,
I think, toward heaven.

A Sure Sign That I've Been Here

You wear your peculiar Aquarian slant
Like a maggot in cupped hands.
Let it eat through, I tell you,
Go ahead and let it eat through!

—Isn't there a downside to all this?
I mean, can I speak in the lisping tongues of PVC
And have birds still land on my shoulder?
Will I be an energy that disturbs no animal?

—Yes, yes, a million times, yes!
Just watch as a rabbit scampers across cyberspace (you know, the *net*),
Watch it ride the thick pursuit of pure electric mind,
A vacant smile beneath a flowering hat

That paints a forest with your face.
—Someone is laughing at my dog,
Someone is chaffing at my God
(The fish-fork of the singing gods)

And it strikes me as a roundabout way of saying something
Like Cliff's Notes to a vigil,
Like a thought bubble that could only read,
"These people have a *bond* maimed *all* the way into the beyond."

A deep green rain falls in hexagonals around my feet
And I feel the future is within me—
—Quick write it in your diary.
—Okay, I feel the future is within me: the vast song, the names.

Over, Under, Through, With

for Rainer Maria Rilke

It is a particle lodged between you and everything,
This fragile pet I hold up to the light.
To watch with soft eyes.
To grant grace to the innocent.

You whistle like a royal bird in morning.
I am nursing a sincere desire,
A maze of species in the green humming of trees.
I see that I am truly my own progeny.

The Apollonian clover-wife sings, *behold in wonder,*
And I applaud the purity of sound.
It is everything I always thought.
But then some kind of revision overtakes me,

Overtakes the ones still out at sea,
And I realize I have cried in rhyme.
I only wanted it to stop and stop,
Not to slide full-force into the heavy grist of things.

I have instead watched my star unravel,
Watched the wisp of an invisibility
Live like a blonde object I have long since put to bed.
And the tree that grows in the ear

Is the apple of my eye,
Over, under, through, with.
I dress the wounds of my unsatisfactory life,
A fallacy that translates all too well.

Beginner's Mind and Purple Plants

Dedicated to the artists of my generation

We eat ice cream at the cerulean zoo,
While saltimbanques siphon the wheat of the whale.
Live wire/wild card, I hold you up, libational,
The dangling factor in a cheap velour equation,
A parade of shiny numeric gestures
Where we become breathless and call it busy.

Brash hours. Penumbral evocations.
The subtle watchbreaker strides along Broadway
Whipped by the chain of Being,
Farting off sequential aromas of the mind-control plot.

But here and there, a certain deadness reigns.
The great swamps blaze,
The great rivers freeze,
And I take great care to notice them today.
Wild branches creep above me
While I am trying to think beneath a damp rainbow.
A muddy-colored rainbow? I can't be sure.

An outdoor vigilance returns:
"Too vitreous. Lacks texture"
"Too textured—no glass"
And the tree becomes something in a window
That I slice up every night.

In all of this, I'm trying to think of what you love,
And how to give it freely, without pause,
How to get inside the tinctured moments splattering
The ghost ship's sails of when we're old.

And I do not *want* the mineral water.
I do not *want* the green green lime.
And I don't want to create what will outlive me
Under an umbrella dripping juice without the squalor.

As for those who cannot out, I can no more speak for them
Than for the handkerchief in the thaumaturgist's hands
That disappears and disappears.

The waffle building—it looks so small tonight.

The planet Dagobah shimmers in the sky.

O where are Chrissy and Weezie and Tootie and Gabe?

Notes

1. The waffle building is the Flatiron Building in New York City.
2. The planet Dagobah is the swampy green planet in *The Empire Strikes Back* where Yoda trains Luke Skywalker to be a Jedi Knight.
3. The series of names in the last line are characters in television shows from the 1970's and early 1980's; respectively, *Three's Company, The Jeffersons, Facts of Life* and *Welcome Back, Kotter.*

Horse Sense and the Evolving Breeze

This double wall of paper dolls is sanctified by light.
An opinion is a mussel, a fact is a clam,
And everything that happens is a spiritual giraffe.

The room is so big and I'm tired of dissolving.
We dream of war, we dream of no war,
An immense, barren liquidity of pelagic spit—

If only we could drink the water and live there.
And if I say, and if I say I love,
In this thirl of venal sun,

Will the xanthic leaves forgive
Their burning autumn hecatomb?
Morning plays once across its golden trumps,

And the sun on the bus makes three of us
As if it were already beyond us,
As if we were any different

In the proem to the feline stars—
O _____ me green with your two-fisted ichor,
_____ me daedal, your painted wings.

I'm the Church You Should Go to More Often But Don't

How I've opened door after door after door
As if to say, I was not sullenly bemused.
Armed choirs. Caprice of a garden.
But I see motive, I see Psyche,

I hear a scoffing Echo blast away the dawn.

Now I am an ex-wife's ex-child,
One speck in a hospitable blur of women
Standing alone on the letter ex,
Stumbling through the halls of geomancy.

Furor Poeticus

The new theologians of a misty sky heed their vocation
To reconstruct a trinity of sterile splendor, based not upon the tall
Indecent failing of straight lines around a hall
Of mirrors that opens into a storybook view of a generation

Anchoring itself to an ill-fated boat
Poised upon a sea, deep as liquid from a vase poured out onto
An almost landless landscape of simple dark silhouettes, a Purgatorio
Where one's personal relation with a wound lingers in the throat.

No, and not upon the artless violence of the Bronze Age
Soaked still in the remnants of a primordial fire, frail
As the nacreous light peeking, as if through a shell,
Through the backdrop of the faltering day. The image

Is, after all, a blind spot, a floating signifier, one
Directly related to the cursive rhythms which call
Us to jostle one another like arpeggios, all
Springing one by one into a post-Victorian

Refrain of reversed figures in a pale array of bowler hats
Of pink, soft turquoise and ecru. Paradoxically, the crises
Which once seemed so vague and sugary now swell with the brightness
Of more fruity colors, sprouting wistfully from our helmets.

Poem Written in 17 Minutes

I write very fast. There is something to this
I think, and the greenness of phosphorescent cities,
How they lick the wind with their swaying tongues
Of smoke. At times I believe they are speaking of me,

"She is a metal girl, rising from the inside of everything,"
And, "Her kissed mercury roots are startlingly chic."
Last week I looked up my name on the Web
To see if anyone shot up anything nasty about my poetry

Lately and sure enough they did. One person called me an "idiot,"
(Re: inept sestinas), said I had drunk too much
Champagne, that my words were a bunch of "bubbly nonsense."
It's a step up; in grad school they were merely croutons.

I take it as a sign I must get very literal-minded here,
To return to that 19-year-old self, who for awhile
Would read only the Polish poets, Milosz,
Szymborska, Herbert, who each had their clean,

Clear ways of working out their relationships to the unspeakable.
But earlier today I went back to Celan,
And for once he didn't scare me. I did not feel
Assaulted by the disembodied suffixes writhing

On the page, I did not hear the hours gasping out
Their last. I saw his words sprawled across
The backdrop of eyes who read and with the same eyes
Watch "The Matrix" more than once, the numbers on the Bloomberg,

Who look to each other for signs of admiration,
And who call themselves Artist. This is beautiful
To me somehow. We have survived.
We're dying, yet we have survived, like dead bridges calcified.
There is blood on my hands as I write this.

Sprich Auch Du

"But keep yes and no unsplit"
– Paul Celan

The big blue blue collar formalist
Ekes out a small cry,
Dry as a cuckoo, tight as a fist,
While suffixes like *-ness* and *-tion* fall from the sky

Like rivers out
Of rain enough to make them rivers, or surprise,
Anonymous volcanoes fresh out of ash.
It is of no use; the aspect is glum, the lines distress the eye

Like a too-sunny day that burns
Right through to the capillaries. I am alone
Here, leaning against a sort of pole. In this scene,
I am an attention, spiraling inconspicuously sideways, then down,

Then, in the spirit of purest mansuetude, up
Into a square reduction of milky, iridescent white
Chaos dancing on the mirage of a lost cathedral until
I'm through. And I am never through, unless my sight

Is somehow severed from my makeshift, rickety bridge. Rome fell
When it was ready. Sodom caught fire.
I can be your house no longer
Than it takes a cheap pair

Of canvas sneakers to bare the beginnings of holes solemnly
At the big toes. What is to become of us,
And you specifically, I can only and extravagantly guess.
The humdrum peaks of forgotten mountains loom dangerously

Now, even as I speak. Clothed in repetitive gestures, the wind
Prattles on. The trees in their bluest morning hour toss
Their rubbery heads among
The streetlamps, transforming the sidewalks into a tautology of crosses

Which, come midday, will have earned their stark and terrible repose.
It's hard for me to understand how eyes can still resemble stars;
After all, aren't we the ones
Who've bombed ourselves and further reddened Mars?

Look, over half of all the saints
Said a lot of questionable things, but no one from those parts
Spoke in parataxes of liquid light:
Something else was oozing out of their hearts

And I think this might be the year
For it, at least I think the night
For Whatever-It-Is to appear.
These days puff like clouds under a plastic butterfly kite.

The Planning of a Park

You dwindle to a blotch of creamy plant food,
And the terrain you straddle is taut and lovely.
If I say, "Leave me alone," you know it means
I will take off in some idyllic taxi

While deigning to absorb your pasty-faced leisure.
Darling, I'm only trying to balance the lack
Of accents here, and I think the solution may be
A good game of handball. You've never played that,

Have you? I promise, the arithmetic after-hunger
Will gown our flowing calves.
Then I could pretend to be an animated Pocahontas
Twirling scrubbed husks over a small fire to dry

And we could get a podium—
God knows you live to riffle through the hymnals
Of the spirit laid bare, and you know I love to sing.
And I'd see to it that the children are well-groomed,

That the talons of their harsh imaginings are clipped.
Hell, I'd even volunteer the sharp moon as a bulldozer
Just to give the trees a proper funeral.
Wait, whose catastrophe did you say this was?

Garbage Art

for Andrew

In the roll-call of succubae
My legs are mated to the new world.
There is no end to this light.
And the power that compels us past devils

Is nothing new. But who threw salt
In my petunias, changed my wine
Into water, who laughed at the vee
Of geese as the day turned its canticles

Of lead? In your eyes I heard
The anti-ballistic bells of summer,
The roar and furor of forced metaphor,
I danced like letters in a two-toned Bible

And paced away from you like a duel
On a seaside. It was for my own good,
It's true. True also that man and nature made me
Their scribe, and now I am a happy drone

Cross-fertilizing the choleric flowers.
A child reads a bedtime story of Armageddon
At a parent's knee, a new day clatters in
Like headsets in an ideal kitchen,

While you dear friend are newly dead.
There are many people around to tell me this
And not one of them is in my movie.
Dear friend you won't decay, won't decay, won't

I Refuse to Wear Life Like a Loose Garment

Waking up from forest-jeering
The apparent Athens is lost forever.
On every blue shoulder I cry.
On every knight-hold I clasp.
Fixed indigo of love plants
On pictures of meat growing darker
        ...jettison...
Listen harder to the unflux.
The parched light of an alias
Wings its way over a dog-eared zero.
And if I say the hunt was good,
Pull me past my time-ridden neighborhood.
Evermore. Ever. Evermore.
My love, where will you sleep?
A velvet Breugel to this Breugel of hell.

Two Poems for Franz Wright

9 Years Have Passed

Only you in a séance of halos,
Only you in piacular bowels stuffed to bursting with pelts,
I want to speak to you finally beyond encryption,
Above the high-pitched cries of the numismatist
Paying for his sin in rarest coins.
Smell of womb abrading the source winding around its loop,
Smell of hunger, smell of gleaming teeth.
In abject wanderings I found how it is to eat nuts like a child,
Found myself in an updraft of fractured things
Riding the brazen highways like a star.

The Sister Hair

Vacuumed the cold bus-light on the intersection, on the ledge,
Boiled the double U of my brain on the heat of its own radio,
Returned transfigured to a swoop of surgeries,
And thought, perhaps this is what death is like.
But what do you call it, brothel of glazed skin,
What do you call it when the mother and the father and the child
Eat from closets enlarged by the loss of scalpels
That cut away tags of ambush?
A shadowy bird traverses a red curtain.
The sister hair. I call it the sister hair.

Color #5

Escape into a road

Tumbling down resin

Eat greens and pork chops

Tomorrow's laughter is the last

To leave me to this place of walls

I never meant

I never meant

I ride out the curiosity of dreamsake

Into a basket case

Of or & etc.

I never meant that it was only here

The Map

for John Yau

I

Lately I have been a victim of my convictions;
That's right, go ahead, laugh.
And in this morning's imperious wanderings
Through the radiator's heat,

The dust from the leaping array of bandaged air
Flecks this parti-colored map of puzzle pieces
I seem to have just driven myself across
On a road of rubber bands.

II

You are the austere beauty of a toolbox
Filled with rainwater, a herd of crayons
Tracing so many trusting circles
Around the degrees of freedom left hanging

From the axes of ignited planets,
Always the dashing alphabetmonger
Strapped to the cover of a dictionary
Pivoting on the wind like a matchbook.

III

You say nothing should be taken
For granted on a pilgrimage.

I say some things don't deserve to explode.

II

Our old proud revel
In runic study
Was to my lips deaf.

In a strange voice
I dove into a wave,
Riding my throat across the sands.

The Newlyweds and the Funny Papers

It was an anagram for something,
Misery I think, that made me want to write
These really eighteenth century-sounding phrases
Like, "the sorrows of the learned"

Or "sleep is emptiness' punctuated sentence."
Anyway, the jumble of bubbled letters was printed in red and blue,
And I found that for the moment it blotted out
The sunny wreck of a morning,

An ax of foam languishing among the circulars
Fluttering into a sea of slow dust upon the stoop.
Wait, I'm lying, I must be, weren't things beginning
To turn around? Please excuse me for one minute

As I must use the toilet. There.
You see you hold the key to my skeleton's forbidden loom
On the days when nothing arrives on time,
When a gaggle of idiots proceeds to laugh

At a broken dream-child in a mirror.
Admit it, it is of no use to anyone, hurling
Those quizzical ashtrays against the wall,
Followed by the parted pleas of ecstasy

Intruding on the paisley light
That is, so to speak, an end in itself
Like a tray of teeny sandwiches swaddled in a tropical subtext.
Can't we just slip it all off, like a cat-suit?

What do the sprinkly statues of lawn animals think?
God these typewriter keys are dirty.
And there you go, drying your hair on the bedclothes again,
As if such magnificence could be said to ricochet

Off our bleakest hours.
Quite possibly, I'm musing on subjects of no consequence,
But I will remain hunched over like this
Until I am encouraged by sleek prophetic words

Seeping under the door like liquid cats.
And this morning further evaporates my worship
Of you, and even its delicate streaks on those bright, huge pages
Display more stamina than my certainty that we asked to be born.

Oh, you have me pegged all right, you who would have me
Fastened to the breastbone of a beggar tufted
All over with a fine down, and surely you would then exclaim
"Hey, that's no beggar—that's my wife!"

In Sunlight

The dust cycles around our happiest moments.
The ones yet to come, that is.

Love, Alters, Everything

1.

In the guided sheen of minus-dreams,
I watch our youth stretched
In the nook of a crossbow,

The heart of a christened fact.
We might as well pry open a snowflake,
Make love in a zero,

In zero gravity, with no one on top,
With the *yeah yeah yeah* of draperies
Shifting in the wind.

2.

Je tombe, tu tombes, il tombe…
From my cyber-garden of Eden,
These Cyclops-tears

Are a stain on your eternity,
An ant carrying maybe-famines on its back,
The ghost rushing for the truck

In your caressed shadows,
Summer on a porch, bottles out of breath,
The sculpted gestures of enchantment's harmonious ark

That splash onto you and onto you my disloyal ink,
The ripped open lungs of my poetry,
This paper-flesh.

Evening with the Financial Report

A chicken cooked under happy circumstances
Is a chicken that lasts forever.
And these various monstrosities that balloon
Under the quelling moonlight reveal the bleakness

Of the two-sided day, drive me to the fringes
Of this cylindrical existence, as we sit
On our tattered couch, futuristically naked,
While bunches of flowers hang

Upside down above us to dry throughout
The length of this long, intelligent season.
Everything here seems reducible to the sawed-
Off light of the candelabrum.

What does it matter if everybody is buying
Out everybody else, who reels in the general
Recession, who pillages, who divests,
Which holders savor the dismal pleasure of 1970's

Supermarket music as opposed to the prurient
Thud of disco pumping itself out of corporation phones?
Tonight I do not see beyond the shiny images
Undulating through your straw-colored hair

Like ants in an anthill, while your chiaroscuro
Eyepatch wanes and finally drops.
At this moment I do not know
How your or my hair will vanish,

How our vows will scatter like November,
How false empathy will be wielded
Like a blowtorch through a box of cake mix
Toward the one of us who survives the other.

What difference does it make, who leaves
The earth first, or second,
If we can continue to catch some of the coin-
Colored reflections of stars turning in the dark-lit sky?

Because that's all we ever wanted
In the first place, and these withered rooms
We rest in, replete with all the small
Comforts of home, will themselves seal

Their warm shadows in envelopes of sunlight
With no return address, scorching over the streets
Of circuitous amplitudes like a firewalk.
"During WW II Bausch and Lomb produced

Over 3 million pounds of optical glass
For the war effort." You sigh,
You, who have always known that the stars

Are the first television, as you fall asleep
With dinner on your knees.

The Maddest Kind of Love

Two retarded men are kicking off their shoes.
Two retarded men are picking through a box of clothes.
How about Thursday? How about Friday?
Duh Duh Duh Duh Duh Duh Duh
Says another man to the lady's head bobbing next to mine.

The sky is hot with sewage microbes.
Saturn returns. Saturn spins out of sight
Past night's reluctant quotients.
In retrospect, it was a grainy afterthought that held us,
Made sense out of things,
And, when multiplied by the barest ceilings of the sky,
Has at times been known to form a golden ring.

You see we're right here at the crossroads
And here I am, angling on my knees.
What are you going to do about that?
I want to know, because when night turns avaricious,
I want to be the one to drape the medal from your neck.
But time is a-racing, time is erasing,
Go and make some sense now, make it!

What do you call those things holding up the bridge?
The moon strums them and we are all its angels.

Life chimes toward me viscerally.

I want to save the world.

The Word Starts with an E

Recall a time when women were vixens.
Recall our honeymoon where we could have made
Sarah or Johnny but didn't.

Bring me your little red ocean,
The twine from between your legs.

And what does the word "plymouth"
Mean to you? Can you snap it
On your wrist as easily as a premium grade rubber band?

Listen, I know you hate that poem about the bicycle,
So I'm writing you a new one,
One that will be a paper wall of sound
While the bees fly by a stone angel on a grave.

The word you're looking for starts with an E.
Not a C not a T not an S not an A I O U Y.
And you my snowy egret, I cannot help you
Until this poem is finished. O.K. it is finished.

Now go ahead: Exhume me.

Consolations Before an Affair, Upper West Side

The ticking minutes shed their sound.
Our ill-matched grammar claps like thunder
Over plates of noctilucent steam.
Strange, you were rich in a poor country
And now you are its mirror.
My catechism was the digital whim of this city.
I feasted on a diet of its most numinous scraps.
It seems neither one of us has obeyed
The edicts of arranged existence.
Earlier tonight I walked here with you,
Unperplexed on the perimeter of what is,
As the nimble sentences springing from your face
Revived my collection of darknesses
Strung around me like a smashed necklace of shells.
Always, this part of the city
Fills with the scent of old ghosts,
And now the tumult of new ones.
For you the undulant tomorrows seem image-laden, plaintive,
And I want to say please, be careful, but I have no right
As your hair is already stricken a little with gray.
I want to find a way to burn it into you from across the table,
Across these fine dressings of civility,
That what I have at any given moment
Is a limbo cloaking my heavy shoulders
Like a balm that soothes the phoenix.

Why We Go To Couple's Counseling

In spite of all common sense, I make my home in the rotisserie
Of your teeth. This was all prewritten on the gravity
Of a giant planet, and those slightly corrupted
Particles of light that formed the stars.
You say the Eternal. The eternal is not mine but has a Big Mission.
Despite our differences, we manage to create a hoax

Of nice weather, an unresolved moment. But the hoax
Is that I search for warmth within the cave of you, a dry rotisserie
Chicken with a mission.
I eat myself and plunge my bones into the gravity
Of crop circles filling with stars.
Our love has been corrupted,

But not corrupted
As one might deem a warped roll of film, a hoax
Of UFO pictures submerged in an ocean of fireflied stars,
But love that hangs on a rotisserie
In a Chinese restaurant, where the waiter brings us our check with a gravity
Whose mission

Is known only to us, who won't be missionary
Later that same night amid readings of Trakl's autumn and black corruption.
Gravity.
What a weighty word! And what if Newton's apple were a hoax,
Nothing more than the stuff in a pig's mouth on a rotisserie
Casting itself up into the stars

To forge a new constellation? I admit, I'm starry-
Eyed when I look at you, every moment seems a mission
Where I am the pig on the rotisserie,
Every oink I oink to you corrupted.
Surely I'm a hoax
And a half laid out in resourceful capsules, but I am in grave

Error if I believe the gravity
Of our rhetoric reaches beyond a drawing of a house with cut-out stars
Above it, some stick figures of cats and children. A hoax
It may be but my mission
Is not complete until I corrupt
All that's been said and search for warmth within my own private rotisserie,

And remember that in the last horizontal hoax of my mission's
Superfluous event, the gravity of my lion paws stretch across the ruins of
the stars
And lie corrupted in your teeth's rotisserie.

A Lived Experience

I sold my eggs. I took a trip.
I mined the ever-lovin' sky
Regularly, at two week intervals.
I listened to its sheer blue business
And saturnine greetings
Falling upon green resplendent fruit.

I'm learning my lessons, learning my lessons.

I stay in my house and make pronouncements.
I have friends, we travel around in a pack.
We sail away in a silken boat
Far from my husband.
Husband, husband, I wear your name like a pageant of shields
While you bandy about, so sad
That I ate compassion twice today.
It's still in my stomach, and do you know,
When I left for work on the Jekyll of the train,
On the Hyde of the train,
Riding into a harbor of intuitive light,
There was the relentless interface of squamous cells
Singing, each to each—how they gleamed!

So I spread my fingers—God was awake.
I closed them—God was asleep.
I sealed myself in watery songs stammering through the tunnel
And raised a fist full of silver at the sky—
All in all, an awesome morning.

Now we're in hell and there's music here, too.
But of all the chants which are chanted in this chanting world,
I prefer the human song that goes:
Why do we have to be sad like this?
Because you're human and I love you for that.

Rondeau

How was I seeing it before? The thunderglass
Was found wanting, the criss-cross
Of anomalous debris. Nature/nurture.
Clocks spin, certain as peace and you,
Too beautiful for love, waste the day's pink odors
On a seesaw of eels. Body,
Body electric, I worship you as the twin

Of all the gone-befores, the halves of all my blessings.
How was I seeing it? The anomalous
Thunderglass, the criss-cross of debris spelled
I found you wanting. And how it was before,
Too beautiful for love, on a seesaw
Of aristocratic eels, I worshipped you.

Winter Dedication

What is truly beautiful never seems to work.
Take, for example, a spider web in the wind,
A great love affair extinguished by mental illness.

But if you hold my hand, we can eat
The saucy food in those cardboard heatable boxes,
We can nosh straight into the driven moonlight

Where a wild turkey marches stringendo
Past the barren trees shimmering on an empty road.
Then there is the issue of stabbing tomorrow

With yesterday's tines, the hasty passages
To destinations. It is terrible, really, to waste the day
That scratches onto our thighs like a prayer.

In atmospheric snowfall, my life barters
Itself for yours (exomologesis and etc.)
And I wear it loosely like the robes of the desert,

So I need to be more than careful, as I reach
Across the fire for instruction
So that I may share this trance with you.

Nocturne

Burnt glass predates sentience.
A waterfall predates * * * *
Clovers descend on the primary light.

Conceived of an immanence and a law,
We liked it that the clocks were wrong.

Proud life splotched with -isms,
Siphoned into molting radiance.

A gun cocked toward the skin of heaven.

An antique indiscretion threaded through
A buttonhole in your shirt.

Drinking back, the choir of leaves
Outside your window's tap tap tap
Is the nuptials' frizzy endgame.

The stars hide in their nylon ruins.

Or

The stars hid their nylons. Ruin.

A piece of dirt dragged through its cures
And causes, and yet but this only my.

One long note into consciousness,
Another long note into snow.

Weird Wife

I wet my lips upon the betterment of the soul.
I look out on Polaris Polaris Polaris
Up from the geodesic dome of purity and sense.
Erotic sanctions. Lunar rafting—

You would not believe the things I go around
Proclaiming from the rooftops,
Waving my hoe deftly at the nearest satellite.
I am a master of a master's master,

A doxy and a dandy on a frond's conquest.
Yesterday lingers on the wall, a fire-flavor,
And the bright formulas we mixed ourselves expire like dead teeth.
I watch you struggle up from traction like a hardy goat,

Shaking pilose spirits from your dust.
For a long time I never went to bed,
Instead, fingering my bifocal eyes, listened to the scintillating kiosks
Through a cage of darkness for a song,

A song of a song's song brimming over a harvest of stars.
Then the symptoms of the planet went *poof!*
Now I play it on my own reveric strings
And plant myself the moon-flowers I lack.

The Raving Fortune

I suppose this is the jumping off point,
Where a skeet, falling from a height,
Cries out, "I guess it was O.K. then, to cross
Against the light," as the lurid afternoon

Reels its aura in. And you, my love,
You've changed, or maybe I have,
And at the rate we breathe in air these days,
I think at any minute that all the bombs should break.

But now I'm laughing, please, tell me about
All the places I've never been, and what the movie
Stars were wearing. Last week at the museum I saw
A man singing "Long Black Veil," my shower song,

While fountains continued to flow in rain
And I started crying, and what's more,
I let you see me do it. The teeth in my mouth
Felt like wet, humped camels,

And I imagined how they must have sounded
In my younger mouth, jangling around like the broken reliquary
Of my child's soul, or should I say my soul,
Yes, my soul, which I sometimes feel

I've shuffled off in favor of this word-life
But then out of nowhere birds fly into me
Making me feel I must be incorrect. Or maybe they think
I am a tree against the watchdog of the open air,

The lusty faces of my palms turned up and ready for their passing rest.
At the baroque concert we endured a month ago,
All I understood of the Rameau was "Le grand malheur,"
And when I heard it, the long ages did not move.

Seconds, minutes, later, I remembered the Greek legend
In which Zeus and Hermes disguise themselves
As beggars and stay the night at an old,
Poor couple's home, a shack of a home,

But a shack where they are warmed, fed, and catered
To like the gods they truly are. And when they reveal
Themselves finally, and grant the man and woman
Their one obligatory wish, they ask only that when it's time

For them to die, they will be allowed to do so together,
At exactly the same point in time and space. When their wish
Is finally fulfilled, it is the gods' will that they are changed
Into giant, sprawling trees, and it is said that to this day one can hear

Their names whispered to each other ceaselessly in wind.
And that is it, my love, that is one version of the raving fortune
That courses through our branching veins.
It raves, it renews, it raves. And with these words

I celebrate the day that will one day fall like quiet
Or unquiet leaves beyond this wordy grid of expectation
Where I wait, as these words can only at this moment be
The phloem of my life, the xylem of my death-in-life.

III

Clothing

I found I had to change into something else
In order to go on
And with this understanding
The long strides of blessing
Came toward me in worn threads

Rushing through the House I Behold the Numinous Dark of Forks, the Light-Bearing Phenomenology of Sunrise

They say the wind was born, bearing its beautiful teeth of light.
They say it is impossible to mingle with a Snuffelufagus
Because nobody else can see it. Nobody could see the prophet
In the man I met, the wandering Christ in long Franciscan robes.
I invited him in and he advised me on semiotics
And the nuances of pop music.

The fact that he stunk to high heaven did not detract from the music
Of his speech, or should I say speech *acts*? It was all in the way the light
Hit the room, bounced off his hair in a just-so way, to invite the semiotics
Of this newest mania into my brain, he was a Snuffelufagus
Having fun with my hell-mind, enrobed
With the fateful words of prophets

Gone awry. In his vision I, too, would be a prophet
Someday, drinking in the reckless breath of music
Like a tray of tiny baritones in oversized robes
Singing "We're in treble now." See, it was all wrong, the light
Was not light at all, it was another bloody sunset where Snuffelufagus
Got sent to the abattoir in an acrostic made of arrows, drooling the semiotics

Of a Rimbaud poem while I did not sleep off the semiotics
Of my newest fancies. Now I have all but forgotten the man, his prophesies
Might as well be oatmeal, O pretty Snuffelufagus,
Take this and eat it, this is my body... You see, I'm on the sentimental fringe of musical
Daydreams, I have dumbed down my brief renaissance into particles of light,
Into doo-wop promises that trickle in among the stars. My robes

Fly open at the slightest suggestion that I've got my lute in hand, and
while I know disrobing
Is the right thing to do, I feel unsure of the semiotics
Of the horse-flavored cheesecake I ordered once in a restaurant, how to
step lightly
Or to have fun with my new mind, flapping up and down its non-proph-
esies
Like a toupee in well-water. Somebody help. I know that music
Won't, the Snuffelufagus

Might, but even the Snuffelufagus
Is making horrible crying noises to go home, wherever home is. My robe
Sweeps the floor of grains of bitterness, a wrecking ball *sans* music.
I know that if I start to take the semiotics
Of my newly-sibilant esses too seriously, I will get varicose zones of
speech, I will fall
asleep in prophesies
Swinging from vainglorious vines, and my mind will not resound into
lute-filled light.

Music is magnificent, splendiferous, whereas the discussion of the semi-
otics
Of my illness is boring. Snuffelufagus, you wear my robes obliquely
As an invitation to the prophets, bearing their beautiful teeth of light.

From Bellevue Aquarium

In the iron-clad crayon box
That works its wonders,
Things are so FU-matic, beyond even that.
The Übermädchen writes her full lips across a wall.

From the window, an eternity of wharves
Peeks out. No lioness is waiting,
No lion claws—foolishness it is!
The water stays good upon its silence.

And me, what am I? I write only what is dictated
To me. Through the holes in my shirt,
My head and hands poke through.
They are trying to keep me comfortable,

On a schedule, on a bare board where I am
Written as the thick soup of the day.

I am No Longer a Mystic

God in a blackout spells ______.
Fashioning simulacra
The tree deposits itself into the soil.
The fires run away.
What is mistaken for coherence
Is merely judgment.
But in your good dream, I am the infertile giraffe—
Pat my neck before I eat
The unfathomable loneliness
Of the ten thousand things.

Try Anyway

My brotherish wounds lace into each other,
Lace around the circuits of Heideggerian light,
Where champagned voices of the undertow
Are subject to angels and Salvation Army trumpets.
I can't hear my own rhythms anymore.
Through the mud of Risperidol, Lithium, Neurontin
And Klonopin, those ugly words which save me,
I sludge, slave to whatever is not cleaned off my brain,
Off my plate, this sky blue sofa
Where I sleep and sleep soundly, endlessly.
Try anyway, he says, and I don't, because
I can't/won't judge the second-hand sky
As my own anymore, its helicopters circling
Like funneled birds that light on the thin skin of my wrists.

The Whole Arcana from the Fool to the World

for Stephanie

I'm tired. I've had enough. But wait—
There is the bridal sound that guessed your fate,
The coded remembrance that parrots the lackadaisical summers
Stumbling into my vision at breakneck speed
On the distended surface of the silence.

My ear is full of orchestras, of shores.

Shh. Lower your voice.
The quiet lines disperse in the halls of some great mystery

And look! There we are (1981) at the root of all fecundity,
Snapping our fingers to the artillery
Of angels who slid off our hands
Into a terrarium full of snakes with names.

How my eye craves you,
How, young, we sneaked past the broadmouthed tasks of time
While the ongoing roads lay in wait for us.
We were alive, alive, hiding ourselves in scimitarical flame,
And our gestures, blindly witnessed, flickered
Against the streets of sky and earth.

Those summers have since reddened in my veins.

Now I go down endless steps.
I shut my eyes like a giant lock.
I recognize a wandering multitude nodding off
To songs of gargoyled umbrage
And I keep walking.

I keep on walking
Down
Down
Down
And every once in awhile I tell myself
It's time to stop,
To pencil in the scantron sheets of no return.

But then I say forget it, it's not worth it.

Now there is lamentation in every street.

Kyrie Eleison

for Joanna

Headache in wine-light
I eat the telluric dark.
Mirror smashed into triangles,

Mirror I whisper into,
Soul of the absent-she,
Thy grass that thirsteth.

I am the anchorite,
You, Pygmalion of the outer limits.
In this razzle-dazzle object permanence

I name the image of the sun
And this, too, is in my memory.
Bromides, this, and the brief charity of worms.

Running with Closed-Circuit Breath

I go out with my judge-face,
Caring nothing for the dazzling plot lines
That rise over me like a vault of moths.
I am scrambling around in someone else's

Daydream, eating sweat, begging for mercy,
Nuzzling through the sweet dilation
Of choral lamps that sing, "And and.
And and and. And and and and."

The bright fingernail in the sky
Dispels the scenery. I used to shine
With it, in full view of all
Who were looking on,

But now, my town has scattered
Like crumbs in a beard, the sun
Is folded up, the she-camels abandoned,
And I, swearing by the stars of retrograde

Motion, wear the seal of musk,
Pant for bliss, and my feet don't develop
Corns on the silk road leading to the silk door,
Tethered to the thread of my unbeing.

Red Poem

Escape hatch blossoming under quilts
The hardware of some dream
Lovingly aches over a small comma
Logic, logic, harmony

The soft alluvial motions,
Life do not, do not continue
This edge of pauses
Terrible inside my throat.

My pulse keeps time
With a torturer's song
Singing everything in stanzas
I slide my hand

Into a ringed syllable
And go somewhere known
But the wing, this wing my body
Is the word on fire, the word

The face I had before I was born

Flashes across a billboard in Times Square.
One could go blind looking at it,
But soon it melts into a thick soup like Dali's clock,
And the plastic number magnets holding up the billboard also melt

Into new, muddy-colored numbers.
Women named for abstractions come to bring me comfort one by one
As I lie beneath the censer-sun
(The same sun blazing across the giant pyramids

Blazes across the desert rising from my heart)
How I would give my face for a clock!
And yet I crave an icon-colored sky,
As I lean, faceless on my hairy arm

Over the day that murmurs like dogs through grass.
I could sing, *That's my star in the form of a hand,*
A hot blue one pulsing with finely-varnished heat
That someone somewhere who lives and breathes

Sees and remembers a light boring down on the edge of the world
With its endless cycles of boys and girls, and of a guiding star
That shines over the blind spot on a fugitive river—
Oh, I would like that very much. Art of days,

Art of nights, I say this so that you may understand
I am at the end of everything, am blessed and cursed in the same breath,
Which is the breathless breath of children flying
Across yards on fire, and still my peace only finds its reason

In the fire that joins the fire of that breath.
Shadow upon shadow, I watch wooden lambs leap out of the void
As a woman lays her hands over my eyes.
Forgiveness? Forgiveness.

Ground Zero, Union Street Subway Station August, 1997

The bulk of us looked on with the risible agony
Of limbless starfish during an eclipse,
A copper emergency slackening its movement.
But you who stood pressed up against me,

You were the skin of a black and white picture
Peeling away the sheen of a winter rainbow,
And you nourished me with your reluctance
To flinch through this morning's privation,

Knowing there is something repulsive about the will to survive
Against all odds, like clawing at the subliminal batons
Of a grand illusion poised between the branches of an olive tree,
The candles of a dark mistake

Blazing in the pyre of the present day.
And if ever I walked the aisle of a sudden plague
Waving a caduceus, I'd trust you to know when I was in trouble.
And if I am myself one day caught bathing in that sweated air

And something in me plummets to its sour demise,
I will be revived by the memory of you, my soldier of fortune,
Who this morning, during the defusing of the terrorist bomb,
Granted me the honor of pick-pocketing my Tao Teh Ching.

Some Meditations on Baboon Living

I saw you through the chit-chat of the day,
Saw you evolving wildly
Say, a new milk tooth, a 50-minute hour, a hyperborean wet dream.
You looked so serious for your age, for any age,
And I felt my heartstrings go pluck themselves
In the way of the beady-eyed uninspired
At the lonesome paradox of self-as-other.
I want to write this down without changing a thing.
Or, I don't want ever to have the need to write this down
But drink in all that I receive
Without complaint or quiet little sob of joy.
You who will hear this, listener,
I hope for your success in all things
But tell me, does this deranged thing
Marked "in use" add to the already formed
Pitter-patter scrawl above the corners
Of your name? Because I'm tired,
And no, I haven't said it all, but if nature
Is the agreed upon ascent toward the good,
How much better it would be were I misunderstood.

I Don't Think I'll Ever Write This Poem

Today I'm slogging over the badlands
In a titanium chalk balloon,
Bobbing like a crouton amid the salad-like winds.
"This is the way of things," I murmur to myself,

A cavernous boast that is host to some edge
Revoking its own penumbra like an order issued
In starkest horror, a rift brittled into a waiting room
Where creepy sequins, pasted with such care,

Fleck and bedazzle the cameo of my supple self-defense.
This is the way of things,
The soft rocks planed down, the wiry thorn bushes,
The love-life with which I learned it,

Forgot it, learned it again.
But I don't think I'll ever write this poem
As today I find I am neither naked nor in love,
So here I pitch my disfigured tent of dreams

And banish this inner parade of relics
From a toy desert where everything lies
Either in wait or to be sold,

A parched orphanage of never-never lands
Where not even these words will go.

Civilization Day

It is nearly always an excuse, never to have done this,
Never to have done that, and it's easier to say
I have this or that to do instead of simply,
I am always in pain. It's true,

If you look at it long enough, (look at anything),
It's true. And the suffering that seems
To come from elsewhere, well, this is
Only the day absurdly hanging its head,

The day that takes the solar road
Past the eulogies that dream us, and it is sad,
Very sad, to think that the flesh is so stupid
That it doesn't even care.

Because vanity is a silver falling forward into life
With its tight jaws and expiating teeth,
A garage to hide its febrile daydreams in while it feeds
On the burning that is besieged. And the false

Vows which destroy me, and which nonetheless,
I carefully pronounce, crowd around to lick
The sores of evening, while someone else
Pulls the lion from the thorn-green sound.

But today is a day to be civilized,
It is Civilization Day! The heat rises
Off the table, the glass moves sideways,
And I run into the rain, of which I speak

So familiarly, and I don't have to do anything
Per se. The Northern Lights still clinging
To my fingers, somewhere I live out my double life,
Yet without the tomorrows hurling through the loops,

And that which has frightened me is dragged
Over the raped earth into the whiteness of spring.
Because time ends in the vagueness of legends,
As my sovereign thoughts remind me that it is the light

That defines us, subtlely seeking its own.
That time I was so helpless—it rises up
In the unmade sheets while my eyes
Go numb across the pleasant plant.

"Poetry is made in bed like love,
Poetry is made in a forest,"
But today is Civilization Day, and my demolished
Dynastic cravings and the statements that are heir apparent

Say, "It depends upon how well one rides
A bucket into the saving grace of wind,"
And so it all goes on in the dangling of a mind.
I could walk up and down this tree-lined

Street for hours and point out what I see:
There are fetuses strung together underground like cans,
Infinitely regressing, there are burning bridges,
There are other things I can't help anybody with.

But today, oh you know what it is,
Today the sky opened up and poured out Kierkegaard,
And his quiet fire dressed my hair, and somewhere I lived
Out my double life; such is the inventiveness of absence.

Meanwhile, I am living a life not to be believed
With a nearness that hurts my eyes, a bird seeking
Successive autumns across the stinging snow.
At other times I'll say, "Press the stop button, press it!"

With the vexed exclamation of the noisy deaths that wake the world.
Mostly I just sit around and watch the rain,
A book of vowels underneath my elbow, and I work in this empty room
Toward some enlightened dawdling, listening for the drill

That will fill the cavity in my heart,
And for the fear that almost broke it open but could not
Or would not make me fall face down upon those inroads
Of infernal mystery to that which has fully come through.

And when evening breathes again into this kitchen
Onto a stack of plates, I will lift up my candle
And join with those who've prayed, I will still myself
And wait for my portion of the brainfood of my surviving days,

Because today itself is Civilization Day,
And though I walk in the valley of the shadow
And though I walk in the valley of the shadow
I have the right to be mortal, and I do what I have to do.

Noelle Kocot's first collection of poems, *4*, was the winner of The Four Way Books Levis Poetry Prize, selected by Michael Ryan. She currently lives in Brooklyn, New York, with her husband, composer Damon Tomblin. In 2001, she received a grant from The Fund for Poetry.